☑ **Y0-DOI-550**

The *Bride's* Book

THE BRIDE'S BOOK is excerpted from a novel,
SURVIVING SIL, by William T.R. Mellon.

Rev. Bill Smith is a pseudonym for William T.R. Mellon.

Other books by William T.R. Mellon
TRYSTS
SURVIVING SIL

Jamie
Once a book person
Always... XX
Rev Bill.

The Bride's Book

(FOR THE NIGHT BEFORE THE WEDDING)

REV. BILL SMITH

SYNAPSE–CENTURION
Santa Monica, Ca

The Bride's Book is a work of fiction.
Any relation to actual persons, places or things is coincidental.

SYNAPSE—CENTURION
225 Santa Monica Blvd. Suite 1204B
Santa Monica, Ca. 90401

Synapse/Centurion wanted to print this book on American grown hemp paper. The Congressional Record is printed on hemp paper every year, but our Congress imports their hemp paper from Italy, rather than make jobs for American farmers and manufacturers. We don't want to cut down trees to make our books. Ask your Congressperson why we have to.

First Edition

Copyright © Keith Kirts 1993

All rights reserved, which includes the right to reproduce this book or portions thereof in any form whatsoever except as provided by the U.S. Copyright Law and permission of the publisher.
Cover Art by Arnold Schifrin
Cover design by Neil Kellerhouse

Publisher's Cataloging in Publication Data
Smith, Rev. Bill
The Bride's Book: For the Night Before the Wedding
Rev. Bill Smith

p. cm.
1. Sexual Advice 2. Humor
3. Questions & Answers
LC 93-84088 1993

ISBN   1-882639-02-2

Printed in the United States of America on tree paper.

2 4 6 8 10 9 7 5 3 1

Chapter 1

Things You Should Know

*N*ow that this revealing little book has fallen into your gentle hands, and you've actually opened it, the secret to keeping your man happy and at home can be yours. All you have to do is follow these few simple words of advice and that part of your life (the married part) can be pretty happy. Happy? Well, happy is an odd word. Most women of marriageable age don't want to go around being happy. One notices, however, that little girls up to the age of eleven are often happy.   Adolescence and womanhood seems to change them.

It's fairly easy to guess that the whole mystery of womanhood is pretty overwhelming. The menstrual cycle alone is enough to make any teen-aged girl edgy and moody, let alone aggressive or despondent. Why is that? Well, it's all twisted up with life and death for one thing. The good old American ostrich society would like to push any mention of death, or life for that matter, under the carpet; but every woman is clearly faced with that question once a month, every month, as the blood flows and the zygote dies—or is fertilized to begin the life cycle. Very raw stuff, this dance of life and death. TV sitcoms, the current teachers of young women, don't address it.

Another part of the monthly blues is that during those three or four days, the crack between the worlds becomes accessible to many women. This is according to Carlos Castaneda. Lots of crackpots use Castaneda for a reference when they haven't done the research themselves. Okay, I admit it, I haven't done the research either. I don't really know about the crack between the worlds. Just the concept is pretty frightening. But I've known a lot of women, and something odd sure happens during their moon times. They get very fragile, almost transparent.   Women need to be loved during those days, but do everything under the sun to be unlovable. Accessing this crack between the worlds without a teacher or a system of laws to understand it is probably damned hair-raising. All alone at the edge of the world every month? Whew! And how many good old American moms can help with this trial? Or Grandmothers? Or Aunts? Not

many. Even though the species has had thirty thousand years
or sixty thousand—150 thousand, a million years?—to come
to grips with this totally natural function of female humans,
we haven't. The male dominator society has pushed this critical, and even interesting, question aside like it has leprosy all
over it. Shame on the male dominators. How short-sighted
can you get? Burning witches, who might have known something useful about women's rituals. Destroying every Goddess
society they could lay their paws on. Tons and tons of information has been lost, so that precious little of this vital info
has come down the time lines. So honey, it's up to you to find
out all about this mystery by yourself. Sound like fun?

Does this question of menstrual cycles have something to
do with a happy marriage? You bet your nipples it does. It's
key. And who else is going to talk about it, if Reverend Bill
doesn't?

If this is your husband's first marriage, believe me, he's
not going to understand why you suddenly start screaming at
him for leaving a few hairs in the bathtub drain, or for watching Monday night football in his underwear. If it's his second
wedding, he might be able to tolerate your erratic behavior;
but he still won't understand, or like it.

So what to do? Now that Planet Earth is seemingly mov-
ing out of the male dominator mode, perhaps into a true partnership situation, we need to work out a practical way to deal
with the recurrent menstrual pitfall.

Certain tribes of American Indians such as Cheyenne

and Shoshone dealt with the menses time by isolating the woman in a separate tent or lodge by herself for the whole three or four days, not allowing her to cook for anyone or take part in ceremonies where her supercharged vibes could affect the harmony of the tribe. They took into account the disruptive quality of the menses and made room for it in their society. I think it would be a mistake to regard these tribes as savages. Before they were hunted down like animals and generally badgered into near extinction, they made incredibly beautiful ceremonial objects and came slightly close to being a partnership society, by all accounts. True, they were male dominant and practiced the arts of limited war; but they didn't drop any A bombs. And they didn't try to rub their enemies off the face of the earth, and they did revere the Earth Mother, and at least made a plan for the women during their time of the month. Maybe it wasn't so bad for a girl to lay around in her separate lodge when she felt the monthly blues coming on. At least she was saved from snapping at everyone in sight. Who knows? I wasn't there. The way we're doing it today, needless to say, doesn't work too well.

My suggestions? Well, before old Rev. Bill became a Reverend, he had quite a few live-in girlfriends. What he found was that none of these fine ladies remembered from month to month that they were subject to turning into weepy rags or fire-breathing dragons. Plain Bill was amazed. It made his life a hell. Occasionally, he would gently mention, "Hey, what's the big deal? Is it your period again?"

Strangely, these gorgeous creatures had become a bundle of hormone imbalance, and evidently couldn't recognize the symptoms, even when these behaviors were obvious to me. How could that be?

Well, how could it? Rev. Bill gets kind of despondent himself, now and then. And so will your young husband. But take my word for it, he won't know what to do when your magical side appears, accompanied by unreasonable tears and bitching.

The question remains, what to do? The answer lies somewhere in the realm of taking responsibility for your actions. There's a novel idea. A young woman being responsible for her actions? Yes. I believe the first decades of this coming partnership world will be a hard go. With women's rights, will come women's responsibilities—and part of that is not tearing your man apart every month. He doesn't need it, and doesn't deserve it—you will admit that, I'll bet—so you have to find a way not to do it.

Anyway, enough of that. Hop on over to a woman acupuncturist and find out about pre-menstrual syndrome. Most acupuncturists know some practical, safe cures, and we can get on to more graspable matters in this booklet.

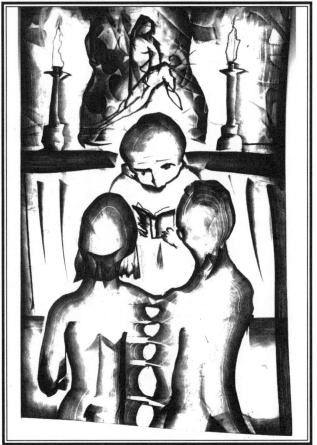

© 1993 James Mathers

Chapter 2

Graspable Matters

*W*hich brings us to the bone of contention in a marriage. This, of course, is the boner, the hard-on, dick, choud, penis, whizzer, weenie, wang, pee-pee, pecker, log, dong, or meat. You, my dear, don't have one of those. Maybe you don't really like the angry red bobber; but if you don't, why on earth are you getting married? Maybe you've been taught by your mother or in church to be afraid of the ugly, throbbing thing; but here's a clue—the love tool is your chief ally. Get used to that idea and life can be pretty much okay.

You own the other half of the human sex machine. And I admit freely that I never met a pussy that wasn't a whole lot prettier than any dick. I am hopelessly heterosexual, or I used to be. Since becoming a Reverend, I'm not much of anything when it comes to the chase. Don't let that confuse you. On the borderline of love and sex, the old Rev. knows his stuff. All I'm saying is I like your pussy.

However, if you're young enough, you may be embarrassed to admit that you adore your own cunning little yoni more than you'll ever love any pecker. Or maybe you've never thought about that. Maybe you're a perfect lady and have never had a carnal thought—and if so I repeat my question, why are you getting married? Peer pressure? Don't you know it's a messy business? Having sex is sweaty and smelly and actually pretty crude. You'd be surprised how crude it can get and still be fun. So unless a little crudity turns you on, it's not too late to run out on this wedding. Keep your finger on the button until somebody who really lights your fire comes along. Be selective. We don't need more babies just for something to do.

But if you've met "the guy", if you're really determined to marry him, here's something to know, and take to heart. He's just as fond of the sensations he gets from his three piece set, as you are of the swirling sensations you get all alone in your bed from rubbing your love nub.

Don't be disgusted or afraid of reading this. I'm not trying to gross you out. This is the real stuff about relationships. No kidding.

Only by knowing the truth, and not being disgusted by it, can you be a big winner at the game of love.

Okay, so here's the information. No woman I've ever known has come to our relationship with this knowledge in her possession. A few of these lovelies have been good learners, and I've taken the trouble to teach them. Believe me, it was a difficult task because they (being women) resisted every step of the way. They just didn't want to know about the stuff that would make me happy. Amazing. I wanted to know everything about their sex organs. I wanted to know a lot more than I could ever find out, even with a flashlight. I was eager to know how to please them! Why weren't they eager to know about me?

Did they think they already knew? No way. They didn't know shit.

They were too shy? Maybe. Women can be very shy creatures, unless they want something. No, actually, the reason was that they weren't interested in really learning how to please me. Why not? Think about that. Why weren't they interested?

Actually, sex is the weak link where marriages come apart. Over 50% of marriage break-up is caused by lackluster sex. Imagine that. Therefore, to keep your marriage from failing, you have to be smarter than your average sister. I will now go into detail about how to be smart about sex. Believe me, it has nothing to do with being interested.

Why People Get Married

Women

A woman gets married for four surface reasons.

1. To better her social position.

2. To avoid being lonely (ie. to have someone to talk to or at).

3. To have babies in a socially and family sanctioned coupling.

4. She is blindly in love. Reason #4 is much sought after, but occurs rather seldom statistically, as a reason for marriage.

Shortly after the ceremony, the bride often wakes up to the fact that somebody has tricked her. Maybe she spends the rest of the marriage feeling betrayed and trapped. Is this drivel? How many happy marriages do you know?

5. There is another reason. Protection. This is a deep-seated cellular reason, harking back to cavemen and cavewomen. This is a "really" dumb reason. Who's going to protect you in this day and age? Nobody on the planet has the vaguest notion

how to protect anybody from A bombs, or hurricanes, or DDT poisoning or drugs (legal or illegal) or doctors for that matter. I don't even mention changing weather, food shortages, invasions of bees or space aliens, or nuclear waste (the byproduct of your hair dryer.) No man can protect you, so forget about that, and learn to protect yourself. Vote the pricks who bring you man-made disasters out of office, and out of public service. Save your children, because these guys don't care about you or them.

© 1993 Arnold Shifrin

Why People Get Married

Men

Men get married for one primary reason.

Oh sure, a few men get married to wealthy women to get an easy ride; but mainly they, as do women, have a deeply ingrained need to procreate during their younger years. The gene pool, way back to the ice age when humans first appeared on Earth, has never failed. Amazing, isn't it? You are the end product of a line of grandmothers and grandfathers that leads straight back to the beginning of human time. So is your future husband. Utterly astounding! Your family tree has never failed to send up a healthy offshoot. That took a lot of fucking over the years. You must come from a very sexy family. So does your young man. Being able to reproduce is a survival trait that has been dominant in your genes, forever.

He has a deep-seated need to reproduce. So do you. This has absolutely nothing to do with getting married. Trust me.

Since he was about fifteen years old, Mr. Wonderful had a lot of pressure, both from his friends and from his own inside self to prove his manhood—to get laid. Take my word for that, too. He spent most of his bachelor life thinking about how to screw a beautiful woman, or any woman. And worrying about why any beautiful woman would want to screw him.

His daydream of coupling occupied his mind all the time, and still does. It floats along beside every other activity he does.

He excels at sports largely so that he can be a dominant male and get chosen for mating by a cheerleader.

Or he excels at the books, hoping to impress a bright female into fucking his lights out. She might be tricked into thinking his dominant brain-power can protect her.

He joins a gang, hoping to get enough social status to attract a woman.

He wants desperately to get laid, even if he's scared of women. Anything he does, women are part of the reason. Why? Because he knows it's going to feel great! And how does he know that? Well, he knows from pulling his pud, while looking at pictures of naked girls, or even making up fantasies about them without pictures. It's powerful. The female form, even in a photo, gives the guy a huge hard-on. Now, that is amazing. He is so conditioned by all those grandfather genes that even a picture of a woman excites him to play with himself. That's kind of odd, isn't it? Why should men and women be so different? We know that young women are much more interested in being popular (whatever that means) than in having sex. Shopping for a new pair of boots is infinitely more interesting.

Anyway, what this young fellow finds out by yanking his joint is that it feels good. Understand that. It feels really good.

And this good feeling builds to a climax. That feels really, really good! All the tension in his body, all his worries about pimples or his job, explodes in stars of bliss. Bliss?

Correct. And he got this bliss from the purple knob of his dick. True, it's a little messy. Milky jizz leaped out the tip and plopped on the toilet seat or on his stomach. But what a small price to pay for bliss, and it's followed by extended minutes of peace of mind. This is such an easy, pleasant thing to do that most men get really good at it before they ever have the opportunity to make love with a woman.

Strangely enough, he knows deep down in his soul that masturbation, no matter how good it feels, doesn't feel as good as plugging into a woman. How could he know that? His genes evidently tell him. His genes are very sexy, don't forget. They keep singing a little song in his ear about how fantastic it would be to orgasm inside a woman. His genes promise to give him gigantic bliss, if he'll help them make a baby.

He could care less about a baby. Believe it! Who needs the hassle of spending all his money on a kid and a wife. But he wants that fabulous bliss! He really wants it. He needs it!

Here's the funny part, his genes didn't lie to him. When he finally hooks up with a woman who will let him do it, it really is great! Even if it's not particularly good, and even messy and smelly, it's great. Great. He falls off to sleep like a baby afterwards.

Okay. That's the background on why almost every male gets married. He wants to be sure he has someone to do this very special act with. Once he's gotten used to doing it, he wants to do it a whole lot more. Every night, twice a day. That's what he tells himself. He won't get bored with sex, or too tired to do it for a long, long time. But he may get tired of doing it with you.

That's where this little book comes in.

Right now, he likes you a whole lot. He likes you enough to put a ring on your finger and introduce you as his wife. He's proud to be seen in public with you, and he pursued you (or at least let himself be caught) and he feels sexy around you. How do you keep him feeling that way? You weren't born knowing how to do that. You may not even know how to have an orgasm yourself. You may think sex is dirty and sub-human. Only shopping, or perhaps horseback riding, is a suitable activity for you. None of that matters. You can fake your way through the bedroom charade every night of your life—women have been doing that for aeons— but you'll have the knowledge of how to keep him sexy and happy and thinking that he has the most wonderful wife in the world.

You're going to be smart. You're going to act like you love his dick.

Isn't that the simplest idea you ever heard? Every single day of your marriage his wong will be there with the two of you, a pretty little doll with a life of its own. And if you love the little guy, every single day, your husband will think you're a smart lady and a good wife, and he won't even know why.

Imagine all the things you can do with a little doll dick of your own to play with. I presume you're adult enough to hear this with an open mind. You're the one who is getting married, not me. You're inviting this third member to the party. Your husband definitely thinks of the short guy as his friend, almost like a small pal who has never let him down. It only makes sense for you to like his friend.

© 1993 James Mathers

Chapter 3
The Secret

*F*orget anything you already know about sex and just keep reading this. You have nothing to lose and everything to gain; because, hey, you don't have to believe a word I say. You're completely free to discard it all, even call me crazy. That's the way it goes with free information. If I was charging a thousand bucks for a weekend seminar, it might be harder to discount my ideas. You would have to act like you got your money's worth. But I'm not giving any seminars, ever. Just this little book, and it's cheap. Cheap booklet, cheap words, right? Just remember one thing, I have a dick and you don't.

Your husband, no matter how fine a guy he is, won't be able to tell you this stuff because he's emotionally involved with you. He might not have thought out the reasons for his discontent as carefully as I have, or he doesn't want to hurt your feelings. He'll just get quieter and quieter, bored and tired of trying to get you to show him some fun in bed, and you won't know what to do. The lovebirds will drift apart, slowly, as the impenetrable walls go up, until they get so high that the only words that come across are, "Let's get a divorce."

Luckily for you, Rev. Bill doesn't mind hurting your feelings. He could care less, one way or the other. Is that a refreshing attitude, or not?

Let's say that you're rightfully disgusted on the first night because he can't do it right. Naturally, it would be better if you weren't disgusted. If you found your new husband's love-making techniques really thrilling, that would be great; but chances are you won't — and it doesn't matter how you feel, really. We're talking about keeping your marriage happily together, at least until you decide to end it. That is a very practical matter.

How you feel during the first week or month or even six months doesn't count for much, because your man will be trying to please you during that time. And he'll keep trying to make you smile until the day when he discovers that no matter what he does, it isn't good enough. Then he'll quit trying. That's the way men are.

Contrary to fable, most men are happy when their woman is contented. Men are born from women. They spend a long time attempting to please their mother. Actually being able to satisfy their loving wife makes them happy. That they often have no clue is pathetic, but beside the point.

Women, however, know from birth that they'll never be

able to please their mother. And they spend their formative years watching Daddy never being able to please Mommy either. Young women get to believing that this is the way of the world.

IT'S NOT. NOTHING IS WRITTEN IN STONE.

To women, the mystery of being a woman is a knowable mystery. But a man can never know about these strange hormonal female creatures, and thus the mystery stays alive— until he is so battered and defeated that he gives up trying to discover all about you. This is what you *don't* want. You do want him to find you eternally refreshing, constantly new—in short, you want him to find the "real you." The exciting, nurturing woman spirit that lives inside you. Well, not quite the "real" you, which is kind of dull and mercenary much of the time, but you know what I mean. The "real you" that you want people to think you are. The actually, pretty wonderful part.

You definitely want him to be there for you when you need him, and the only way to make fairly sure that he'll stick around, is to be there for him when he wants you.

So what batters him, and what props him up? What, exactly, makes him feel like a well-loved man?

Here's a secret. If you are disinterested in sex, eventually he will be disinterested, too—in having sex with you.

No man, who is whole in any way, ever looses the desire to drop the love torpedo on an attractive woman. Even old men. Sexual desire starts out being body desire, but with age it often progresses to mental desire. Mental desire, at least to some degree, never goes away. It seems to be hooked up with manhood. Let's assume he finds you attractive, both mentally and physically. If he doesn't, he's marrying you for your money. Stop the wedding!

But if he digs to be near you, and wants to touch you all the time, and his whizzer gets hard just from touching your hand, it's a pretty safe bet that you turn him on. If you keep turning him on for a year or so, he will really fall fully in love with you. That's called sexual bonding. It's the trick that the human race uses to keep families together—to keep the man hunting or farming or getting up for work every morning, so his wife and children can eat. If you can make the bedroom into his safety zone, chances are his love for you will turn into armor plating against the advances of that pretty secretary.

Hey, no man is perfectly faithful, given the right circumstances, and no woman is either—but what have you got to lose by trying this simple, simple trick. Learn to love his dick. Fake it at first if you have to, but be gentle with it and learn to like it. Be playful, but don't make fun. His dick will try to make you happy by standing at attention like a warm cucumber—your own body-temperature dildo. You can learn to pleasure yourself with this devise. You can get him to fuck you the way you want it—if you're smart enough to learn how you like it. Some women actually do like sex. You might be one of them.

But, even before you learn to love the little guy, you do need to handle it. That is critical. Touch it gently, sweetly, as shyly or as boldly as you want to. If you take the initiative with his sex equipment, you'll be amazed to discover that you're in control of the bedroom.

"When you've got 'em by the balls, their hearts and their minds will follow." That saying is attributed to some right-wing dictator, but he was right. A guy will do just about anything to keep your sweet little hands on his dick, if you do it right.

Here's why this technique works. The human race is constituted with the amazing ability to have sexual orgasms. All the higher mammals have them, too; but humans have evolved, or were given, the desire to have them all the time. Most other animals, except some primates and bears in captivity, don't bother with orgasms until the female goes into estrus. But humans will truck along gratefully orgasming 365 days a year.

Rev. Bill would like to assume that you have this happy ability yourself. However, some females are stuck in this area. Their upbringing is so shallow, that this critical part of life is suppressed. There should be classes in orgasming taught in school and in churches, as was common during the Goddess epoch; but instead, everybody has to sneak around and learn it for themselves—and think they're weird because they want to. Well, maybe they are weird, but orgasming is a species survival trait. Those who do it freely, have more children and pass on their genes—those who are stingy about it have a smaller selection of mates. That's the way it is, and has been for a half million years or so.

How Does That Affect Sweet Little You?

Well, it's your choice. I'd say you definitely have the genetic ability to bond with a mate by orgasming together; otherwise, your gene pool wouldn't have made it down through time to this late date. If you can learn to climax with your husband's member in you, then the marriage has a real good chance of success. I know it's fashionable for doctors to suggest that your clitoris is in the slightly wrong place, or at the slightly wrong angle for penetration orgasms, but let me put it simply. Bonding is a kind of addiction. The human race addicts to all kinds of things. If you get addicted to screwing your mate, it makes for a strong bond. Simple, no..? But getting your kicks from his snake is fairly difficult, unless you like the way it makes you feel. Like it very much. Wow, what a great gadget. Better than a cucumber. Much better, because you can't get a cucumber to take the garbage out later.

The Male Member

Here's the thing about the male's sexual implement, it's very sensitive. In all ways. Remember that, and you won't have any problems with him in bed.

Many unknowledgeable women grab a dick and pump it fast and hard, like a jackhandle that they're in a hurry to get pumped up. Like they're angry or afraid of it. They think it's made of steel or something. It's not. It's as sensitive as your clit; in fact, it's the same organ (kind of.) You might want to think of playing with a dick (or at least the head of it) in the same manner that you massage your clitoris. Does that make the issue clearer? I trust that you have touched yourself.

It is possible that a circumcised dick is a tad less sensitive than a natural one with the skin covering that keeps it moist and lubricated. But that doesn't mean that a guy with a cut one likes to have it yanked by harsh, unskilled hands.

Then why doesn't he complain?

Ah, there is the recurring dilemma. Most guys are afraid of offending a woman, who beyond his wildest dreams has agreed to jump into the sack with him. He doesn't want to drive her away—and it's mighty, mighty easy to offend the thin-skinned darlings. Women are as thin-skinned as a dick. They get hurt very easily.

Have I said enough about this? It's very important. He wants you to touch him, but he doesn't want to be hurt (except in the rather rare cases of male masochism.) And he doesn't want to be bitten during an oral episode, or scraped by your teeth.

Exceptions to Every Rule: If you are very skilled at sex, or if you learn to be skilled, the tiny biting and scraping techniques described in the Kama Sutra and elsewhere can be very pleasurable to him. But no unconscious, blundering in this area, please. He probably won't tell you that you're hurting him (that would be unmanly) but he will be less enthusiastic about visiting your bed. No kidding. If he sleeps on the couch, you're doing something wrong.

Maybe I'm all wet about this subject of sensitivity. Lots of women all over the world are too rough, in my estimation. That could be why they were still available to fool around with old Rev. Bill, instead of being happily married. Or maybe my liturgical weenie is more sensitive than most, but I don't think so. In locker rooms and during coffee breaks every place I've ever been, some guy is talking about Lucy Lu or Sally Jean who "grabbed his cock so hard he thought she was going to jerk it out by the roots." Really, dear, this is a very common complaint.

Pregnancy
and How to Keep Him Paying the Rent

Okay, so you get married. Let's say you and the big bruiser actually have a great time for the first few months, or even longer. Just like you thought you would. You go out to dinner now and then, and party on the weekends. Your sex life is pretty good and shows signs of getting even better. You're starting to trust him. And then—then you get pregnant.

That's great! Having a baby is most of the reason you got married. Hubby may not know that. He thought you were crazy in love with him. Maybe you thought so too, but your survival genes wanted to have a baby. Remember, they've been doing that, mother to mother, for at least a million years. And your genes want you to continue the survival game. Since you turned thirteen and had your first menstrual cycle, they've been dinging in your ear, "Have a baby. Babies are nice. Have one." So, now you're going to.

Meanwhile, Hubby is out in the cold. He feels stranded, in spite of the fact that he's supposed to want this baby. He's unloved suddenly, and mostly unwanted. Why? Because you make him feel that way. Your hormones are spasming up and down, your whole system is out of control. You act like a hormonal idiot. Your genes want this baby, but you are nauseous, and probably even frightened because you don't know

what is going on in the body you've come to depend on.
Yours. And you definitely don't feel like being nice to your
nice guy husband. He is such a slob, always hanging around,
pawing you—trying to act attentive, but he's so insensitive to
your real needs. He even wants sex!

He's a barbarian. You scorn him. He crawls off alone to
a bar, to lick his wounds. Those wounds are real! His best
friend and playmate doesn't like him anymore. The world has
collapsed. Nobody can help him. He doesn't even know what
he did wrong.

What actually happened is that you left the poor boy
stranded. The safe zone he has come to depend on in the bedroom has gone South. Gone sour. He blames himself. He
blames you. Communication disintegrates and the perfect
couple starts to drift apart. Probably, you never get back
together like you were in the beginning. The trust just isn't
quite there. Eventually, the Big D looms on the horizon, with
the promise of leaving you alone with a baby. And I don't
mean Dallas, Alice.

Changing this scenario is so simple. A smart, practical
lady like you will understand right away. Keep on playing
with his dick. This ain't going to kill you. Even if you're sick as
a dog. So what if you toss your cookies, you will anyway. Even
if you're totally repulsed, you can spare the little guy five minutes of relief. I mean it. Every day during your pregnancy.
Remember, you've already learned to give him a beautifully

sexy hand-job—doing it takes almost none of your energy. Why destroy his harmony and safety for no reason, except your laziness and self-centeredness?

Do you think cavewomen grandmothers had the luxury of flaking out on their manioc gathering duties just because they were pregnant? No way. Neither should you. Why send hubby looking for somebody else to play with? That's stupid. Give the guy a break, and he'll realize that you're a really good sport. Trust me.

Of course, at a certain point in pregnancy, many women begin to feel really sexy themselves. They want to get it on with the mailman and the grocery boy—and sometimes they do. Why not? They're not going to get more pregnant.

Hubby was shut out of the bedroom some weeks ago, before the sexiness kicked in, and now he's hopelessly confused. Kind of like a yo-yo, bouncing up and down. Now you want him, now you don't. He's spending a lot of time in the bathroom, probably jerking-off. But you're horny, suddenly. Tough luck. You damaged his delicate psyche*.

* Note: *The male sexual psyche is much more delicate than most women's.*

Another myth exploded. Here's the truth. The race has survived because women aren't really very delicate. You know that, and Rev. Bill knows it. And I'm saying that men may scratch and fart and act like the worst kind of pigs; but you can make his dick shrivel up to nothing by making fun of it or acting disinterested. So if you don't want him to pout, and don't want him eventually to go away in search of his True

Love—don't make him feel unwanted.

That's just about the end of this lecture. Pretty simple, really. It's up to you, darling.

There's just one more thing. Read lots of books, the best ones you can find. Good novels and new science. Both of you. If your minds don't keep growing, marriage stagnates. If only one of you reads, then that one will drift off in search of intellectual stimulation. Sexiness actually begins with a quick and curious mind. Golly, that sounds liberal and dangerous, doesn't it? Not a bit. The New Age is coming. Be part of it. And tell a girlfriend about this little book.

Chapter 4

Questions and Answers

*T*hese are a few interesting questions that Reverend Bill has been asked in his role of advisor to brides. Most are about behavior after the wedding. The answers are self-explanatory. Rev. Bill invites you to ponder these imponderable questions.

Sara J: Do you think he'll be a good provider for me and the children?
Rev. Bill: (small chuckle) Reverend Bill isn't a psychic, dear. If I were you I'd certainly think about finishing college.

Diane S: Why do women stop wanting sex after they get married?

Rev. Bill: Have you been married before?

Diane S: This will be my third. I really want it to work this time.

Rev. Bill: Well, marital sex is a very complicated question. Brides are as surprised as grooms are when the sex stops.

Going back through history, we find that women want to make love with heroes as a reward for being heroic. This is ingrained in all tribal situations. Heroic actions, usually by males, keep the tribe from being destroyed. Heroism needs to be rewarded. A banquet followed by sex is a normal prize.

Nothing much has changed down the years, except that heroes are vanishing—to be replaced with a sham courtship consisting of an "exciting heroic" movie, following by a hamburger at the Malt Shoppe and then sex. Unfortunately, there aren't enough heroic movies to last a lifetime, not even on TV.

During the conquest of you—the act of catching you— even a dull guy was transformed into a hero for the length of the courtship, because you are a very special prize, to you and to him. Well worth climbing mountains and swimming oceans for.

Why doesn't he remain a hero is the real question. You demand heroic deeds so that you can feel good about bathing his wounds and then screwing until his eyeballs wobble. But modern life isn't set up for heroes. Taking out the garbage isn't heroic, neither is watching television. There is very little about sucking for promotion or keeping your mouth shut about the chief's blunders that can be termed heroic. It's hard to act like a hero in the face of belittling wage earning.

Bathing his aching, smelly feet after a day at work isn't exactly what you had in mind when you thought of tending his wounds. Is it? Listening to his petty gripes is a turn-off, not a turn-on. Even if he's a trial lawyer involved in protecting the rights of the unprotected—a real gladiator—even then the day to day stuff will be deadly dull and the feet stinky.

During the courtship, he was aimed at you. All of his stories and amusing anecdotes left out the parts that made him look dull or venal. Of course, your stories were slanted to make you look good, too. After the conquest was won, he realigned his sights—at his job probably. He was aimed at that before—until the heroic distraction of you came along and lighted him up. It lighted you up, too. Why, oh why, have you stopped looking up to him? Why don't you want to fuck?

Well, the truth is you do want to. You'd like to fuck the mailman or that cute guy at the office. But you expect more from your husband than a quick roll in the hay. You want a hero, always aimed at you like he was during the courtship.

A practical suggestion. Reverend Bill has noticed that about the worst time for relationships is the hour after he comes home from work. He's beat. He needs to unwind from the dull routine. He wants a shower, needs to take a dump and rest his feet. He needs to shift gears into the evening. If you would give him an hour to have for himself when he gets home, you'd be surprised how much better things might be. That means not yipping at him to fix the sink, not explaining in detail all the perishingly dull things you did with the geraniums. Nothing. Smile and leave him alone. Or better yet, be out shopping.

If you work, too, it's a little more difficult. How can you both get out of the way during the unwind time? Some couples solve this problem by working different shifts. With that arrangement, it is possible to see your love object quite seldom. Some of the strongest marriages are set up this way. The lovers come together for sex now and then—basically as often as she wants to—and they don't drive one another witless with stupid war stories and complaining. And they still have national holidays together.

Diane S: Did that answer my question about why I quit wanting sex after I get married?

Rev. Bill: Well, basically, I'd say you don't choose men very well. That's the hub of it. Why don't you take a close look at what might make a man stay heroic to you.

Diane S: Okay.

Rev. Bill: Well...?

Diane S: Well, I try to pick out men who....well, the first time I married a really great looking guy, but that didn't work out because he didn't want to make much of himself. I was probably too young, and after that I had Timmy to look after, so I needed a man who had a decent job. It just seemed better to have enough money. I don't know, it's so hard to find a shining knight in all the areas that are important.

But that's not it—I had really good sex with every one of my men! We took trips together. Really, Reverend Smith, I was hot for every single one of them before we started living together. I love making love. One time I even went to the acupuncturist to see if he could calm down my sex drive.

But as soon as I get married, or even start living with a guy, the sex evaporates. To tell you the truth, it's just awful. Within a week or two, I can hardly stand the thought of letting him touch me at all. Honestly, I really want a permanent, loving relationship. Every time, it seems like it's going to be perfect, then it turns to dust.

Rev. Bill: What did the acupuncturist say?

Diane S: (coy smile) I don't think that's your business.

Cloe L: Why do women turn into witches as soon as they get married?

Rev. Bill: That's a peculiar choice of words.

Cloe L: What is?

Rev. Bill: Witch. Maybe you're onto something there. When a woman gets married, she simultaneously gains power and loses power. A witch by definition is a woman who has certain power—kind of a natural power, a ritual power. Up until recently, this whole area of women's power has been quite misunderstood; and I'm sorry to say that the Church has been largely responsible. For the life of me I can't understand why men (and the priesthood of most religions) suddenly became the enemies of women, but they did. Very short-sighted, since women are the mothers of all men. Strong women generally produce strong children and a strong future. Now the pendulum seems to be swinging again. We'll see how it works out.

But back to your question. I presume you meant why do women get bitchy and bossy as soon as they get married. Well, they all don't, for one thing. There are plenty of mousy wives who creep around being subservient to the slob—hoping in that way to keep the marriage together. Both the bitchy pose and the mousy pose are caused by the same modern phenomenon—the family unit has to be run as a business.

When you, dear, are on your own, in your own apartment, you run your own business. When you take in a partner, you expect that partner to pull his own weight—but he was undoubtedly used to running his business differently than you run yours. Friction happens. Most couples don't talk about division of responsibility before they get married. His priorities are seldom going to be the same as your father's, or even yours. It takes a few years to get straightened out. In the meantime, you both go slightly nuts, because you find that your partner (not your employee) is sloughing off on the responsibility that you think is important. It's really difficult to be nice to a partner who you think is dogging it—so you turn into a carping witch. Where's the problem in understanding that?

The difficulty is in changing crappy behavior. That takes

inspiration, or divine intervention. I, personally, find that divine intervention with the household budget is a wish that will likely go unanswered. You might pray to stop being a bitch, but getting that to work might keep you on your knees the rest of your life. My suggestion? Learn how to fix that leaky faucet yourself, or get the guy next door to do it. Grow up. You don't have to hate him, just because he won't rake the leaves. He probably didn't rake the leaves the whole time you were dating.

Nicole Z: I've been married to Andrew for about a year. We get along really great together. But his job takes him to New York every other week. Phil, his best friend, lives here and he likes me, too. He always liked me, even before Andrew and I started dating. Phil and I are friends. I love him, but I don't feel romantic with him at all. My best girlfriend, Simone, really digs him; but he doesn't like her, he likes me. Simone is starting to hate me, but I didn't do anything to keep her and Phil apart. If they got together, I'd love it. Why does stuff like this happen?

Rev. Bill: You lucked out, Nichole. This is an awkward situation; but if you were hot for Phil it would be even worse, wouldn't it?

Nichole: Would it?

Rev. Bill: Trust me, having an affair with your husband's best friend leads to bad feelings, sometimes even tragedy.

Romance is a hodgepodge. To tell a perfectly handsome and intelligent man that you have no interest in ever sleeping with him is not fun; but it certainly isn't a tragedy.

Your girlfriend, Simone, is the sore spot in this whole episode. I don't know why people tatter themselves with this kind of stupid jealousy decade after decade. It seems to serve no purpose. Attractions, false and real, are going to happen. Women are going to sleep with men no matter what stands in the way, if that's what the gene pool wants. Why do friends have to get bent out of shape with jealousy? Of course, that is the question you asked—and I don't have an answer for it. Sorry. You have to live as honestly as you can in the face of your attractions, and other people's attractions; and if friends fall by the wayside, you just wave good-bye.

You aren't leading this Phil person on a little bit are you?

Nichole Z: I don't think so.

Rev. Bill: Good.

Lynn W: Everything I thought was cute about Ralph became extremely annoying after we got married?

Rev. Bill: It makes you want to scream, doesn't it?

Lynn W: It makes me want a divorce. I feel like such an idiot. The thank-you cards aren't all sent yet, and the marriage is over. I think I'm cracking up. There is nothing wrong with Ralph. He's the same. I thought he was so witty; but it just isn't funny the third or fourth time you hear it.

Rev. Bill: I'm not certain, but I think assembly lines, auto-mobiles and television have caused your problem. When you go into the back country areas of the world, people still talk to each other. They have time, and they need to communicate because getting neighbors to help mend a fence isn't the same as hiring a handyman. We in the city, with all our time saving devices, don't have time to turn around—and our talking and storytelling reflects this lack. What does Ralph do?

Lynn W: He works for Boeing. He's an engineer.

Rev. Bill: Is it noisy at his work place?

Lynn W: I don't know. I've never been there.

Rev. Bill: You've never been to the place your husband works? Incredible. This could never have happened if we hadn't left the farm. Not that the farm was so wonderful, but you see what I mean.

Lynn W: It's restricted. He took me to a Christmas party in an empty hangar.

Rev. Bill: (snuffs in disgust) Look, Mrs. W, I would love to help you with this problem. I mean it. If I could upgrade the bore quotient in this country, I'd snap my fingers and do it in a second. Way too many people, men and women from all economic levels, laugh along with TV sitcom laugh tracks. Automatons. Passive automatons is what they become. And our government and industries encourage the dulling of the American mind. Don't they? Evidently they do. The business of America is business. Everyone at the top says so, and what business wants is a compliant work force—people who don't mind being numbed-out by their job. (Laughs.) But you want a man who doesn't bore you to bits?

Lynn W: Yes.

Rev. Bill: Good luck. Even in the back country, TV watching is taking over.

Kim M: Why did I dress up to the max until the day after my wedding, and basically I haven't worn anything but sweat suits since? I don't think this is very bright, but I feel comfortable in sweats.

Rev. Bill: Personally, I think sweat pants can be very sexy; but if you have a problem with them, it's easily remedied. Throw away your old sweat suits and ratty bathrobes. Out the door, into the recycling bin, now. Not tomorrow. Right now. You don't need them to clean the house or wash the car. Wear something else.

An alternative to sweat pants is baggy silk or satin harem pants. Those definitely are sexy. Of course, you will want to keep up your exercise plan whether you have sweats or not.

Wanda B: Then there's the trust issue. If you're five minutes late, they don't believe a word you tell them.

Rev. Bill: Do you mean jealousy?

Wanda B: Maybe. It's like I screw up his schedule forever if I'm a few minutes late.

Rev. Bill: You're seeing this from the female point of view, which is fine; but from the male's, there are a couple of issues here. One is that men have been responsible for the safety of their women and children for aeons. Granted that this job is collapsing—your man can't really keep you safe from a car wreck while you're speeding to your meeting with him—but his inbred response to you being late is to worry. He'd rather walk down to the river bank to see if you fell in. Or maybe jog up to that grassy rise—if he caught a glimpse of you being chased by a bear, maybe he could save you. But hanging around in a restaurant waiting, or even watching TV at home while he's waiting for you to show up, takes away his natural male proclivity to do something about finding you. It's pretty much impossible to find you in a city, even if you might be in trouble—so not knowing what else to do, he stews. Then when you come waltzing in, all smiles, he snaps, "Where have you been?" Then he growls for twenty minutes.

To calm him down, you are forced to go into a minute by minute travelogue of why you were late — which most generally sounds like a lie even it's the truth. Sometimes it is a lie, and maybe that sounds more like the truth—but the moment of meeting is kind of broken.

As far as jealousy goes—if he finds you attractive, he will probably imagine that most other men are trying to get into your pants. Jealousy, although hateful, is very natural. Women (and men) find it convenient to lie about where they've been rather than face jealousy. This always backfires, given enough lies.

Let's touch on why women lie. You could say it's all

right to tell a few lies—as long as you're not lying to yourself. And maybe it is. During the last two or three thousand years of male domination, women had to lie quite a few times to escape severe punishment. They've gotten good at it. Lying to then is second nature. Men are so ponderous and non-verbal. Why the heck do they have to know every little thing you're doing? Where's the freedom in that?

Correct. There is no freedom without trust. What you need is a paradigm shift.

But until the shift occurs, the problem with lying is that you might become known as a liar to the man you're trying to have a life with. As ponderous and non-verbal as he is, his genes remember tracking a deer and catching salmon in the rushing river. That means that sooner or later he'll track you down and snare you in a lie you can't escape from. If he cares enough to track your lies, he'll catch you, because lies leave a trail in the ether—and if he loves you, he's hooked onto your vibrations. Besides, you're not a very good liar, not really. At the moment of catching, he'll know you're a liar, and he won't trust you. Rest assured that he has experience with a woman who lied to him before he met you. He doesn't want to believe that you'd lie—that's partly why he's ponderous. But now, he's gone and caught you.

Women are trying to bootstrap themselves into a better position in the coming New Age. My advise is not to overlook this lying thing. It's not cute. It's not really good for your soul. In fact, it's only forgivable at all when you're under the thumb of a slave master or some other form of dominator.

Right now we're all on the cusp. It's unclear what the

shape of the New Age will be. If you think you might want to have a partnership society, lying can't really be part of it. To break the cycle of distrust, stop lying. Telling the truth and demanding the truth is empowering. Lying and accepting the lie ruins everything, eventually.

Of course, truth telling isn't always easy. I'm embarrassed to admit that I have told a few lies to make myself look good. What a colossal embarrassment. My face turns red every time I think it. Why did I lie? Opened my mouth and out it came.

I have even told lies rather than hurt someone's feelings. It didn't do any good. Their feelings got hurt subliminally by the lie—and they didn't get honest info to mull over. They didn't think better of me for copping-out to the lie. In the end, it was hurtful all the way around.

On the other hand, tactfulness is never wrong. Bludgeoning a friend with the truth is not charming.

Hope C: Is it possible to reconcile after you have a miserable break-up?
Rev. Bill: What do you think?
Hope C: (beseechingly) I want to.
Rev. Bill: Well, I never heard of a relationship coming unglued when both parties were armor-plated with love. Unfortunately, love wears thin; then the door opens for heart-

break. What happened in your case?

Hope C: I met someone else, and it confused me. He seemed like my soul mate.

Rev. Bill: I'm not surprised. Your marriage seemed solid; but it was always up to you, because you have stronger energy. Lou is much more placid. Is he moping around waiting for you to come back?

Hope C: (rolls eyes) Hardly. He's having the time of his life. Taking vacation trips with young chickees. Skiing, Hawaii.

Rev. Bill: Meahwhile, you've been out in the world checking out the available men. You realize you had a pretty good thing going?

Hope C: I never changed the way I feel about Lou.

Rev. Bill: I understand. That's the problem. You thought of Lou as a good catch and a potentially good father and a pleasant companion. It worked for quite a few years; but you were never blasted with love. Were you?

Hope C: I thought I was, but I guess not.

Rev. Bill: I'm not saying you had to be. I suppose you followed my advise about not lying?

Hope C: Yes.

Rev. Bill: (shakes head sadly) You said something like, "I think I found my soul mate?"

Hope C: Yes.

Rev. Bill: The male ego is so stupidly delicate. All these years, Lou undoubtedly believed that he was your soul mate— whatever that means.

Hope C: What *does* it mean..?

Rev. Bill: I have no idea. These cute pop psychology terms don't seem to hold up for the long haul.

Hope C: (quietly) I didn't sleep with him.

Rev. Bill: The new guy?

Hope C: We didn't. It was just intense and confusing. We started a neighborhood project together. It was very intense.

Rev. Bill: Evidently. Well, your question was about getting back together. When you break a ceramic pot, is it possible to glue it back together? The pot might appear to be fixed if you're careful, and it might even hold water; but truthfully, it's full of cracks. A marriage is the same as a crockery pot.

But if you're serious about getting back together, you might try begging, "I made a big mistake," or something like that. You'd be on probation for at least several years, maybe forever. I don't really think you'd be able to put up with that. It would probably lead to a lot of fighting. And besides, your friends would be uncomfortable. Basically, it would be pins and needles. But try it. Why the heck not?

On the other hand, your bargaining position would be much better if you wait for him to beg you to come back. He might. You caught him before, and he has even better reasons now than he had then.

Hope C: What reasons? I'm not as young as I was.

Rev. Bill: No, but this divorce is going to cost him a fortune, isn't it?

Hope C: I hope so.

Rev. Bill: Playing hard to get *is* frightening. He might forget to ask you to come back.

Hope C: I'm petrified that he won't.

Rev. Bill: Sorry, dear. Life is full of risks.

Finally

In spite of all these pages of advise, I don't really know much about women. That is probably evident. Or about men either for that matter. We are kind of a mysterious species.

I hope you're having joy with your love affairs, whether married or not. Sex and love are meant to be pleasurable, in spite of the fun I might poke at them. When all is said, relationships are probably the great teachers—better than Himalayan gurus. With so many people having relationships, it's surprising we're all not enlightened.

And finally, blow jobs are not the critical factor that you may have heard they are. I've never known them to make or break any relationship. So if you're worried about that, don't worry. Soap and water makes the whole issue of oral sex more appetizing; but mainly just roll with what turns you on. It's kind of easy, if you've chosen a human being to do this intimate stuff with.

Acknowledgements

The publisher wishes to thank to following people for help above and beyond the call. Elizabeth Porto, Cindy Malloney, Idelle Steinberg, Flin Kirts, Steve & Ina Lapin and Gary Fisher for proof reading and editorial help. Neil Kellerhouse for typesetting and cover design. James Mathers and Arnold Schifrin for letting me share their drawings with many brides. Ilene Fogel and Katy O'Harra at Gemini Graphics, who printed this book. Helen Taylor Sheats, Karol Rainier, Dan Cytron, Michael Goth, Jeffery Curry and Robert Matthews. Without all of these people this book would not have happened.

*Sex without love is like a tree
without flowers. Of course,
trees come in many forms.*

*There **must** be more to the*
New Age than lower back pain.

Terence·McKenna

*I knew Jose Mondragon wouldn't
go through his entire life without
attempting one great thing.*

Ruby Archuleta

© 1993 Keith Kirts

ORDER FORM

Telephone Orders: Call (310) 829-2752. Have your Visa or MasterCard ready.

Postal Orders: Synapse—Centurion
        225 Santa Monica Blvd. Suite 1204B
        Santa Monica, California 90401

Please send the following books. I understand that I may return any book in new condition for a full refund—no questions asked.

How many

The Bride's Book by Rev. Bill Smith $6.95

The Devil's Drainpipe by Keith Kirts $9.95

Space Sex by Keith Kirts - coming 1994

Shipping: Book Rate: $2.00 for the first book and 75 cents for each additional book.

Air Mail: $3.50 per book.

Sales Tax: California residents add 8.5%

•Check   •Mastercard   •Visa

Card #...

Name on card....................................Exp..../.....